The big

Story by Beverley Randell
Illustrated by Ernest Papps

Dad kicked the ball,
up, up, up.

"Oh, no!" shouted Dad.

"Oh, no!" shouted Tom.

Tom and Dad
looked for the ball.

Tom and Dad
looked and looked.

Tom and Dad
looked and looked
and **looked**.

Tom looked up.
"I can see the ball,
up in the **tree**,"
said Tom.

"Look at me,
up in the tree,"
said Tom.

"Here you are, Dad,"
said Tom.
"Here is
the ball."